Contents

Background ....
What Green Plants Need To Survive 2
Fertilisers 5
Using Keys 6
Information Overload 10
Recognising Animals 11
Information Cards — Common Oak 12
More Information Cards 13
Food Chains 14
Different Plants Need Different Things 16
Looking at Different Soils 18
Animals and Plants Suit Their Habitats 20
More Food Chains 23
Big Food Chain Questions 24
Revision Questions 25
Index 26

Answers to the questions are on the back of the Pull-out Poster in the centre of the book.

This book covers unit 6A from the year six scheme of work

Published by Coordination Group Publications Ltd.

Contributors:
Angela Billington
Chris Dennett
Lindsay Jordan
Tim Major
Katherine Stewart
Claire Thompson
Tim Wakeling
James Paul Wallis
Suzanne Worthington

ISBN 1-84146-277-2
Groovy website: www.cgpbooks.co.uk
Jolly bits of clipart from CorelDRAW
Printed by Elanders Hindson, Newcastle upon Tyne.
Text, design, layout and original illustrations © Coordination Group Publications Ltd
All rights reserved.

Background

You already know loads about plants and animals. This page'll give you a quick reminder about plants.

I want to know what happens to plants if you keep them in the dark. I've done an experiment with three identical plants. I kept one plant in the dark for 12 weeks. One was in sunlight for 9 weeks and then in the dark for 3 weeks. I kept the other in sunlight for all 12 weeks.

Q1 These pictures show the plants after the 12 weeks. Using the words on the notepad, write on each plant's label what state it's in, and how many weeks it was kept in the dark.

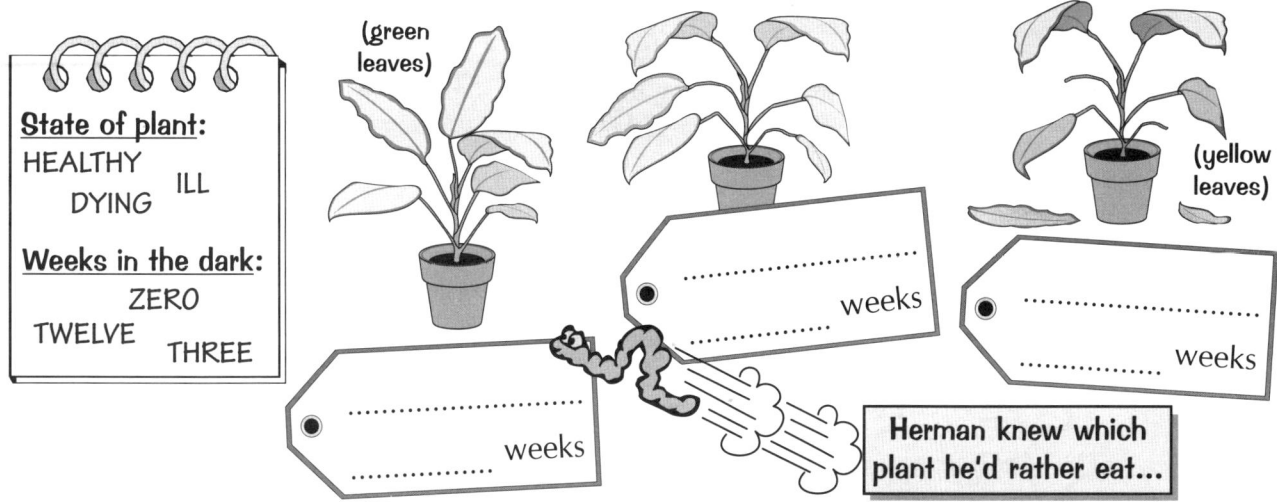

State of plant:
HEALTHY
DYING   ILL

Weeks in the dark:
ZERO
TWELVE   THREE

Herman knew which plant he'd rather eat...

Q2 After the experiment, I wrote a conclusion. I've written it below, but I've left some words out. Fill in the blanks with words from my computer screen.

holidays dark
light three
twelve five

The plant that was dying had been in the dark for .... weeks.

The plant that was in the dark for .... weeks wasn't healthy but should recover. To be healthy, a plant needs ....

Q3 a) This plant is healthy. Look at the picture, and pick out the three things it needs to <u>survive</u>.

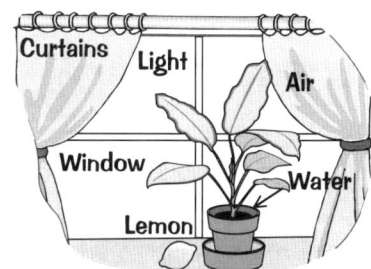

① ....

② .... ③ ....

b) Here's a list of the three things a healthy plant has that help it <u>grow</u> well. Fill in the missing letters to finish off the words.

① H .... L T H Y L .... E S

② A S T R .... G S .... M

③ H .... L T H Y R .... T S

Turn over a new leaf — go to page 2...

You have to <u>look after</u> plants. If you ignore them, they'll soon start <u>losing leaves</u> and <u>eventually die</u>.
And don't forget outdoor plants — they need exactly the <u>same</u> things to survive and grow well.

What Green Plants Need To Survive

You can tell if a plant is healthy by looking at it. If you give an ill plant what it needs to survive, it will <u>grow</u> and <u>change</u> to become healthy again.

I left my sister's favourite potplant in my cupboard for three weeks. I was doing an experiment but she's not very pleased. To get myself out of trouble, I've got to make it healthy again.

I need to get to the root of the problem.

Q1 What three things are essential for the plant to recover? Tick the right boxes.

Cup of tea ☐   Light and warmth ☐   Carrot ☐   Water ☐   Air ☐   Music ☐

Q2 Straight away, I put the plant on a window sill. These pictures show it over three weeks. After three weeks, the plant has changed. Write down two changes in the space below.

First day   1 week   1½ weeks   2 weeks   3 weeks

Change 1 ....

Change 2 ....

Hint: One of the changes is about stems.

Q3 Look at the last picture of the plant after three weeks. Is the plant healthy again? ....

Q4 Oops — I came back from holiday and realised I'd accidentally left my own plant in the cupboard for 3 weeks. What will happen to the stem, roots and leaves after 2 weeks if I take it out of the cupboard?

....

....

....

What music do wilting plants like — heavy petal...

You can recognise a healthy plant by its <u>strong stem</u>, lots of <u>green leaves</u> and <u>healthy roots</u>. If you stick a plant in the dark it might recover — but it <u>might not</u>. It just ain't nice, so don't do it.

What Green Plants Need To Survive

Green plants need light, water and air to survive. If they don't get any one of these three things, they will become ill. Luckily though, plants are usually pretty tough and can recover.

Vaneeta and Duncan have done an experiment on their school playing field. They pegged two sheets of plastic onto green, healthy grass. One sheet was black and the other was clear. Here's what the grass looked like when they took the sheets off after five days.

(pale yellow grass)　(green grass)

Q1　Why was the grass yellow underneath the black sheet of plastic?

....

....

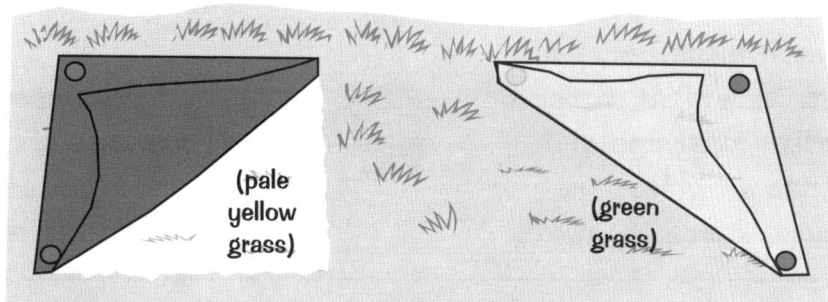

Vaneeta put cotton sheets on her flower bed.

Q2　After the black plastic was taken off, what would happen to the grass if it was left for a couple of weeks?

....

....

Q3　Fill in the blanks in these sentences about plants. Use some of the words being poured from the watering can — you won't need all of them.

Plants use .... , ... and .... to make new plant material.

.... , ... and .... are all types of plant material.

water, sheep, pot, soil, air, roots, stems, cement, fabric, tools, light, leaves

Yes, OK, I did it — don't grass me up...

Green plants go yellow if they don't get enough light. The healthy green colour shows the plant is using the light. Different plants are different greens, but it's always to do with them using the light.

What Green Plants Need To Survive

A healthy plant needs <u>nutrients</u>. The plant in the picture below is getting everything it needs to be healthy. Read the information around the plant then answer the questions.

The plant makes new plant material using air, water and light.

'Plant material' means any part of the plant. 'New plant material' means new leaves, stems and roots, and new growth on the original leaves, stems and roots.

Green plants turn light, water and air into things they use to grow. They do this in big, flat, green areas that work like miniature factories.

As well as light, water and air, plants need small amounts of nutrients, which they usually find in the soil. Just like humans, plants need nutrients to stay healthy.

Q1 Which parts of the plant are "**big, flat** and **green**"? ....

Q2 Fill in the blanks in this sentence using words from the blob below.

Without .... , the plant wouldn't be able to make .... , ... and .... into the products the plant uses to ....

Blob words: air, change, soil, light, heat, leaves, cola, water, grow

Q3 a) Why do plants need nutrients? ....

   b) Where do plants usually get nutrients from? ....

   c) Which part of the plant takes in the nutrients? ....

Q4 What two things does the plant get through its roots?
   Hint: you've just answered a question about one of them.
   ① ....
   ② ....

Mouldy pancakes — they're big, flat and green...

Plants need <u>nutrients</u> to survive. Most plants take these from soil using their roots. Plants don't need the soil itself to survive — just the <u>nutrients</u> in it. Fertilizer and 'plant food' contain nutrients.

Fertilisers

OK, this is a bit confusing. You hear people talk about 'plant food', but as you know, plants <u>make</u> their own food, so what's going on... Well, fertilisers for plants are a bit like vitamins for us — they are essential, but they are only a <u>tiny part</u> of the food that's needed.

Here's a bottle of fertiliser... 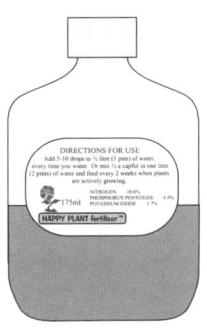 ...and here's its label.

DIRECTIONS FOR USE
Add 5-10 drops to ½ litre (1 pint) of water, every time you water. Or mix ½ a capful in one litre (2 pints) of water and feed every 2 weeks when plants are actively growing.

175ml
NITROGEN 10.6%
PHOSPHORUS PENTOXIDE 4.4%
POTASSIUM OXIDE 1.7%

HAPPY PLANT fertiliser™

Here's another 'plant food' label.

1 Litre **TOMOFEED™**
Liquid tomato fertiliser — for high yields of top-quality, full-flavoured tomatoes.

HOW TO USE
Dilute 20ml in 4.5 litres of water.
Apply diluted feed to base of plant.
Under glass: feed at alternate waterings.
Outdoors: feed every 7-14 days.
Growing bags: feed once a week.

Nitrogen	4.0%
Phosphorus pentoxide	4.5%
Potassium oxide	8.0%
Magnesium oxide	0.03%

WARNING!
Don't touch plant fertiliser. It has nasty chemicals in it.

It was smaller than me this morning!

Jackie had put too much fertiliser on her plant.

Q1 What chemicals are used in <u>both</u> fertilisers? (Don't worry, you don't have to learn the names.)

....

....

Q2 Does a plant need huge amounts of fertiliser or tiny amounts?

....

Q3 Complete these sentences by writing in the right words from the brackets.

Plants make their own food in their .... (LEAVES / FLOWERS) , using air

from all around, water from the .... (SOIL / AIR) , light from the

.... (MOON / SUN) and nutrients from the ....

(BIRDS / SOIL). Animals .... (CAN / CAN'T) make their own food, so they

get food by .... (EATING / BREATHING IN) plants or other animals.

Firty lies — that's an awful lot of lies...

Giving a plant <u>fertiliser</u> (the so-called '<u>plant food</u>') will make sure it gets the <u>nutrients</u> that it needs to make food with. If you don't give them fertilisers, then they'll have to get it all from the <u>soil</u>.

Most people spell it 'fertiliser', but some people spell it 'fertilizer' — both are OK.

Using Keys

Keys are diagrams that help you tell what something is.

Q1 Use the key on the bottom half of this page to identify these organisms. Write the name of each organism next to its letter.

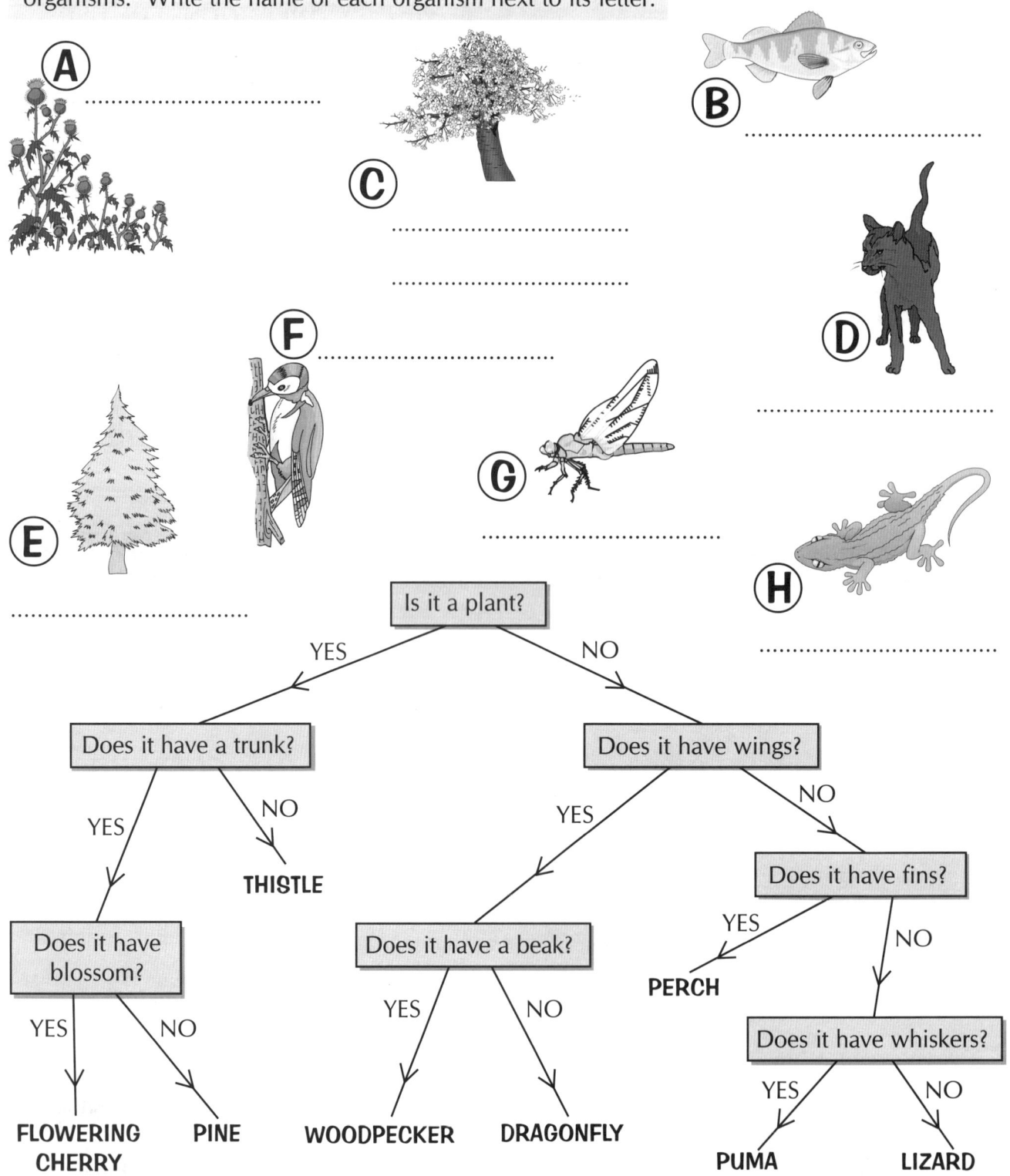

This page is the key to your success...

Keys are really useful — and they're not as complicated as they look. All you have to do with this one is go through it for each organism, answer the questions and follow the arrows carefully.

Using Keys

Here's another key — to identify something <u>different</u> this time.

Q1 Janet is walking along a muddy path and sees some animal footprints — but she doesn't know what animals made them. Use the key below and write the animals' names beside the prints.

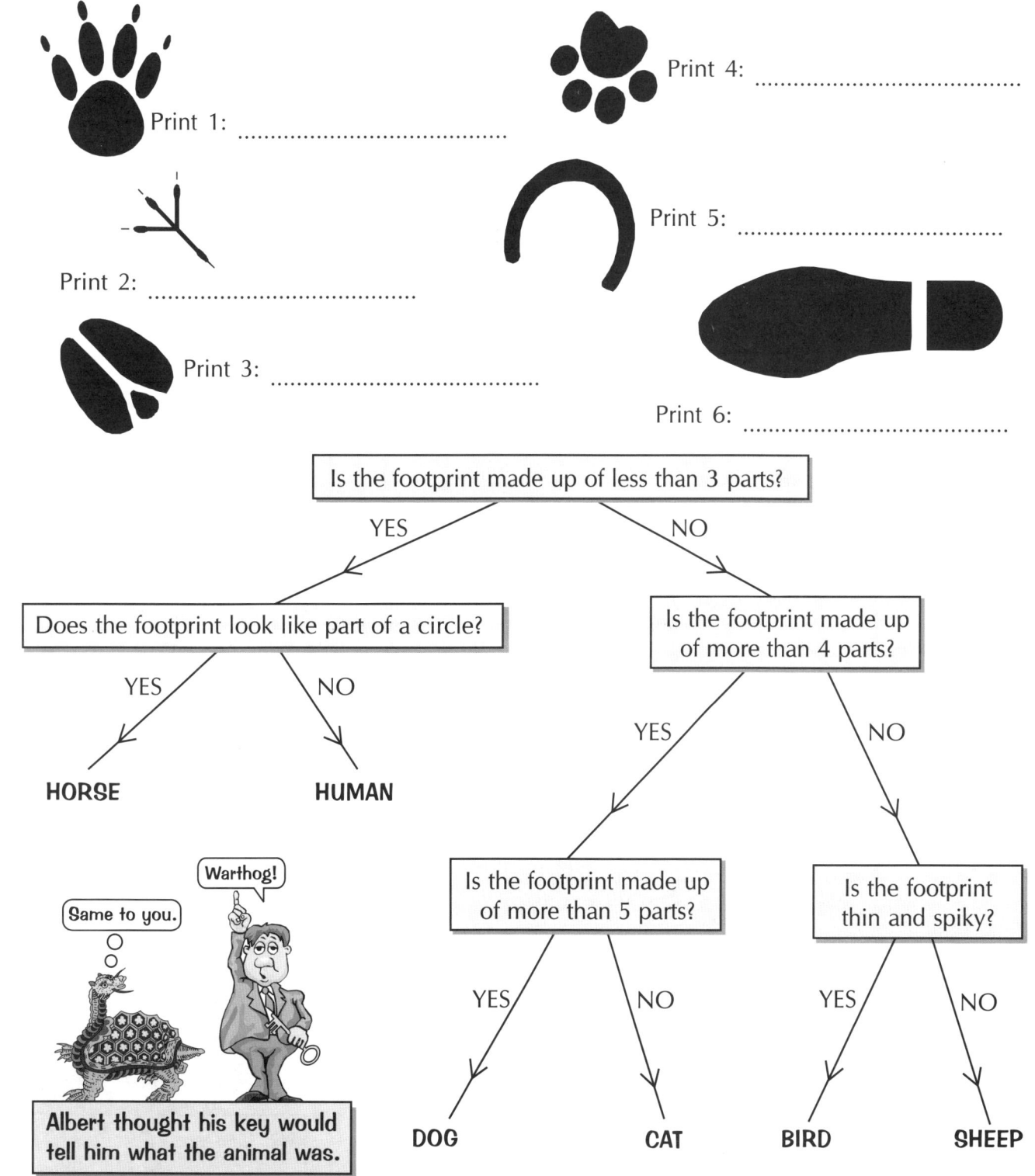

Print 1: ....
Print 2: ....
Print 3: ....
Print 4: ....
Print 5: ....
Print 6: ....

Albert thought his key would tell him what the animal was.

Footprints — what policemen ask animals for...

The best way to use the key is to do <u>one</u> footprint at a time — go through the <u>whole key</u> for that print until you find what it is, then do the next footprint. Don't do too much at once or it'll all go <u>wrong</u>.

Using Keys

If you know the <u>names</u> of the organisms to start with, you can fill a key in.

Q1   This key isn't finished. Write YES and NO in the right places next to the arrows, and write the animals' names in the right places on the key.

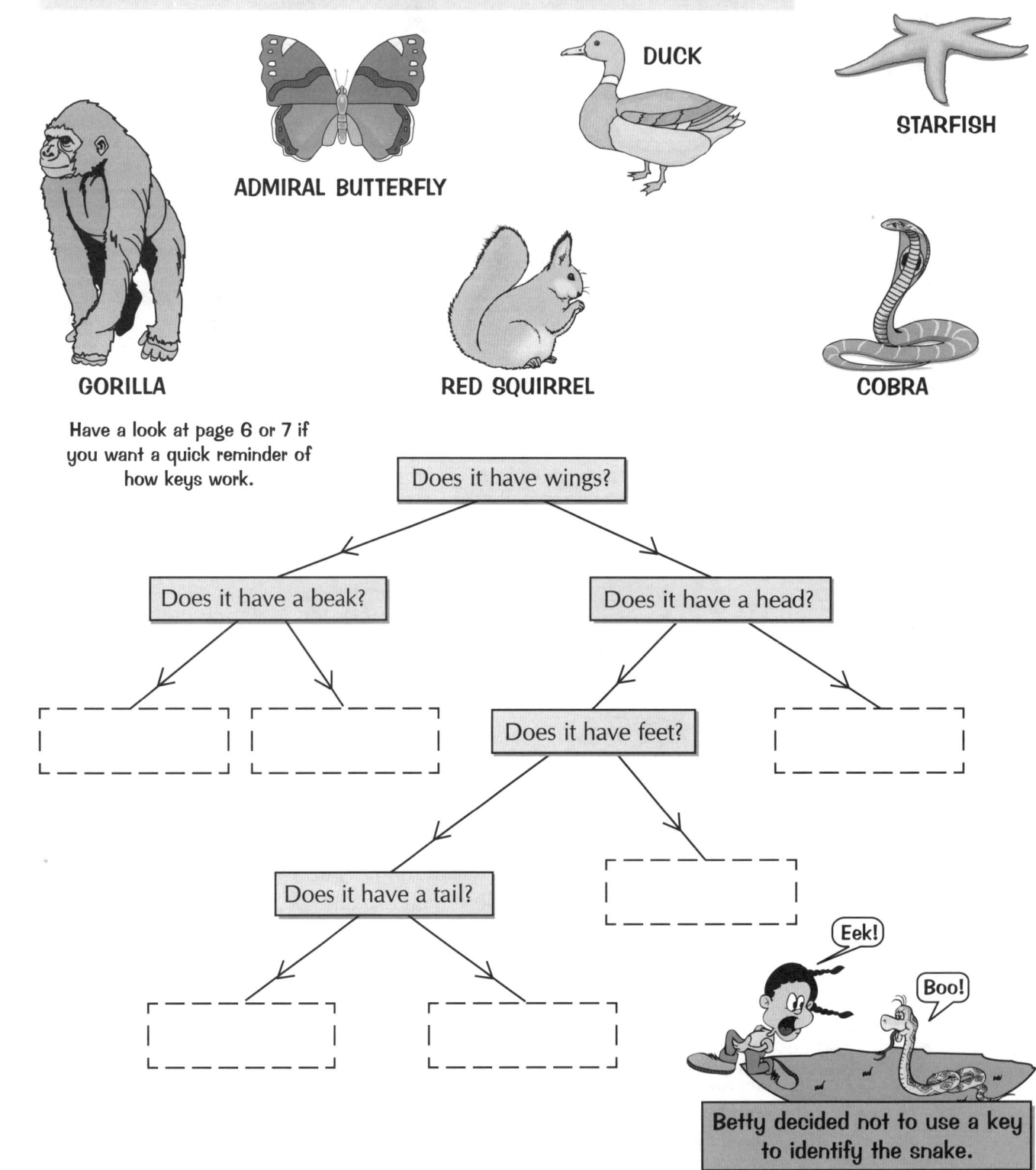

Have a look at page 6 or 7 if you want a quick reminder of how keys work.

Betty decided not to use a key to identify the snake.

How does a gorilla open doors? — with a mon-key...

Sometimes they like to get you to <u>make</u> the key yourself. It's not hard — just do each organism <u>one at a time</u>, putting 'yes' or 'no' until you get to the end, then write the organism's name in.

Using Keys

You can make a key yourself — but do it carefully, and make sure it actually works.

Q1 This time you can make your own key — I've only given you the organisms and their names. You need to fill in the questions, the YES and NO bits, *and* the names at the end of each branch. Keep the questions simple, and make sure that all the organisms go into the key.

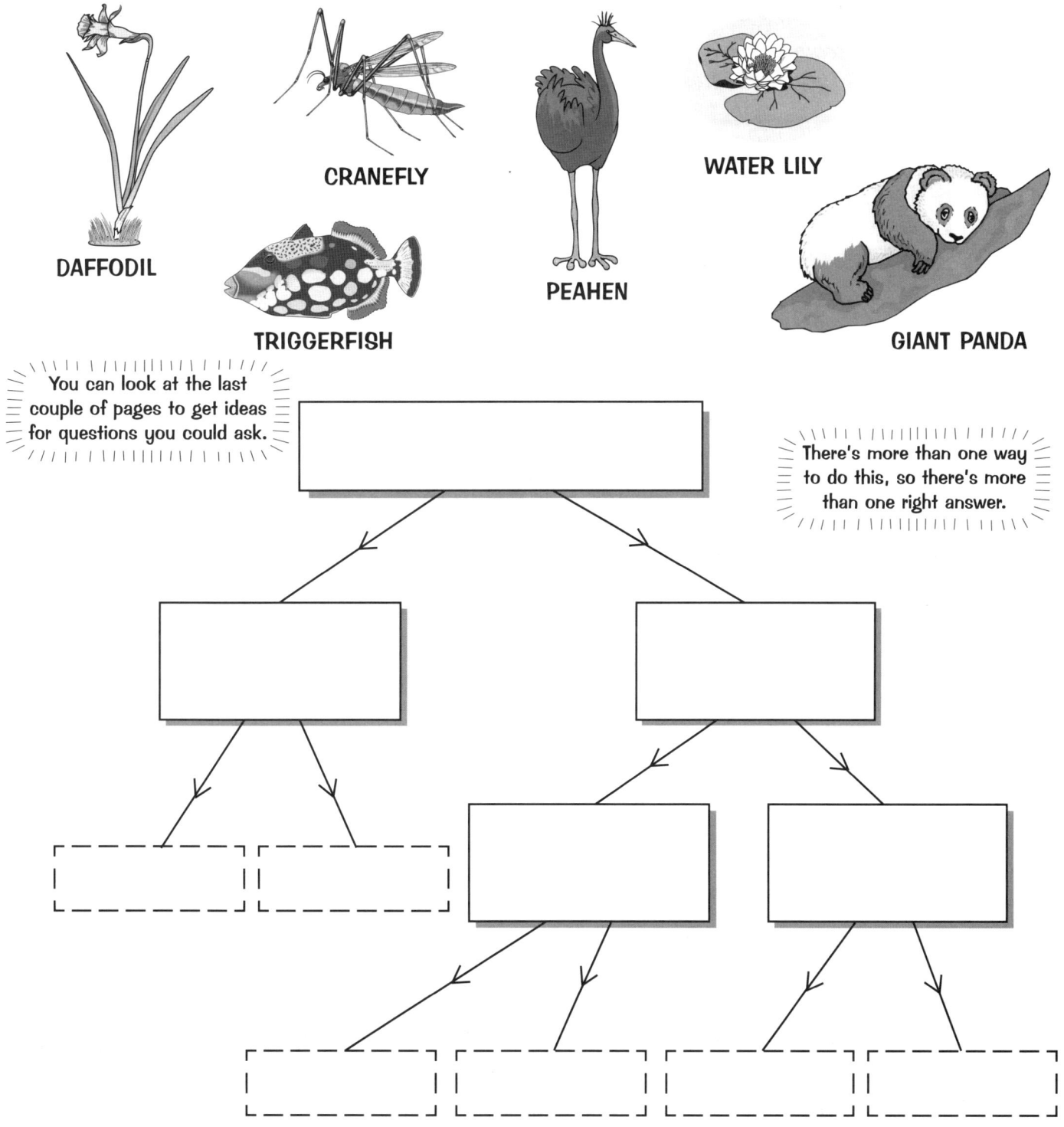

DAFFODIL   CRANEFLY   PEAHEN   WATER LILY   TRIGGERFISH   GIANT PANDA

You can look at the last couple of pages to get ideas for questions you could ask.

There's more than one way to do this, so there's more than one right answer.

I'm all keyed up for yet another key joke...

The way to be really sure you've got it right is to try it out afterwards — pick an organism, go through the questions, and see if it gives you the right answer. If all of them work, it's right.

10

Information Overload

Nothing to <u>write</u> on this page, but by heck there's a lot to <u>read</u>.

Q1 Read all these bits of info — from note book to web page. When you're done go on to page 11.

Field Notes - Tuesday 19th June

I've been watching the pine martens for several days. They are fantastic climbers and agile too. They often leap from branch to branch using their tails for balance. They mainly eat squirrels, but I've also seen them eat a rabbit and young wasp larvae. The family of martens I'm watching are living in the hollow of an old oak tree.

Dear Mum & Dad,
Summer school is great! Today we learnt about foxes and how they live in families in burrows called 'dens'. They eat things like rabbits and voles. We read a book by Roald Dahl called "The Fantastic Mr. Fox" and it was brilliant. Tomorrow we're gonna learn about squirrels, but I already know they eat acorns and live in trees. WISH YOU WERE HERE!!
Love from,
Martin Pine XX

600

mead /miːd/ n. an alcoholic drink of fermented honey and water.

meadow vole n. ORDER: *Rodentia*, FAMILY: *Circetidae*. Small rodent commonly found in meadows; feeds on grass and seeds. [vole originally *volemouse* from Norwegian, from *voll* 'field' + *mus* 'mouse']

mealworm n. the larva of the meal-

Barn Owls in Decline

The amount of meadow land at the edge of farmland has been greatly reduced. Meadow land is the ideal habitat for meadow voles, which are the Barn Owl's main food.

The last undisturbed areas of meadowland are those alongside major roads. This means that many are killed by traffic while hunting near these roads at night.

The British Barn Owl (often found nesting in old farm buildings) is in trouble. Without intervention the wild Barn Owl population of Britain will be completely wiped out.

INSECT FACT FILE

No. 23 Oak Apple Gall Wasp

- Gall Wasps are parasitic stinging wasps. Scientific name: *Biorhiza pallida*
- Scientific classification: The gall wasps are in the family Cynipidae, order Hymenoptera.
- There are over 1250 species of gall wasps worldwide — living mostly in northern temperate regions.
- Oak apple gall wasps lay their eggs in the bark of oak trees. The wasp causes strangely shaped galls* to form on the bark where the eggs are laid. The wasp larvae eat the galls and live inside them until they grow into adults.

*Galls are strange-looking bumps that are a bit like warts. The galls on oak trees are called 'oak apples' and they are an actual part of the tree.

Internet sloth web finder - [yawn...]

Address http://www.notarealwebsite/greenwoodpecker.ht

The Green Woodpecker
picus viridis

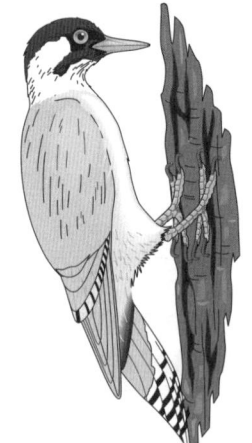

A bird more often heard than seen, the Green Woodpecker can be heard drumming for insects in the bark of old trees, or calling with its distinctive "yaffle" cry. They build their nests in old, high trees (such as Oak and Birch) and live off a diet of insects and larvae (e.g. bumble bees, gall wasps and beetles).

All woodpeckers have a pointed bill and a reinforced skull to allow them to drill into the bark of trees to find insects. There are fewer woodpeckers around today, due to the simple fact that there are far fewer old trees around for them to live and hunt in.

Meadow Grass

- Wind pollinated.
- Seeds distributed by passing animals. They stick to fur and fall off somewhere else.
- Grows on meadow land.

Recognising Animals

Read everything on page 10 and then answer the questions below. Some of the questions are quite hard — so you'll have to read the info carefully and use your brain a bit.

Q1 Write in the names of the organisms below. Use the info on page 10 to help you.

= ....   = ...

= ....   = ...

= ....   = ...

= ....   = ...

Q2 What is a gall? ....

Q3 What two things make woodpeckers suited to drilling in bark to look for insects?

i) ....

ii) ....

Q4 Name two animals from page 10 that live in the same habitat.

Name of habitat: ....

Names of the animals: ....,

....

Q5 Describe how meadow grass seeds are distributed.

....

....

No matter how many times his dad told him, Rocky had to learn the hard way.

Recognising animals? — well, my sister's a pig...

This page is all about finding the information you do need from a load of stuff you don't need. Much easier than finding a noodle in a worm farm, so no moaning (unless you're a noodle).

Information Cards — Common Oak

This page is all about finding the information you need and using it to answer questions. Here you'll find out about the wonders of the <u>Common Oak</u>. A rollercoaster ride of knowledge for sure.

Q1 Read the info card about the Common Oak tree and answer the questions below.

COMMON OAK

Scientific Name: *Quercus robur*
Tree Type: *deciduous (loses leaves in winter)*
Flowers and leaves: *produced in May*
Pollination: *wind*
Seeds: *acorns*
Seed distribution: *Squirrels bury acorns to eat later. They forget about some and these grow into new oak trees.*
Nutrients: *From rotting animals and plants + animal waste (e.g. Deer poo).*
Provides food/home for: *Young Gall Wasps, Squirrels, Birds.*

a) What are an oak tree's seeds called? ....

b) Describe two ways in which oak trees rely on animals.

....

....

c) Describe two different ways in which animals rely on the oak tree.

....

....

d) What does 'deciduous' mean? ....

....

Q2 Write down one more fact about oak trees that's not on the card. Use p.10 or an encyclopaedia or other fact book about trees to find it out.

....

....

The mighty oak was lucky to survive the mad rabbit attack of '98.

Why did the Oak have footache? — he had A CORN...

All the information you need is on the page (well, nearly). So all you've gotta do is <u>find it</u> and <u>write it out</u>. After that lot it must be time for a break...   ...right, that was long enough, onto the next page.

KS2 Science Answers — Plants & Animals in Their Habitats

Q2: Food chains always **START** with a green plant because they **DON'T** need to eat anything. Green plants make their own food from **LIGHT**, air, water and **NUTRIENTS**. Animals need to eat food to survive and don't make their own, so there is always something **BEFORE** them in the food chain.

Q3: Food chains always start with a **PRODUCER**. Anything in the food chain that eats something else is a **CONSUMER**. An animal that eats another animal is called a **PREDATOR**. An animal that is eaten is called **PREY**.

Page 16 Different Plants Need Different Things
Q1: Buzy Lizzie and spider plant.
Q2: Giving the plant nutrients.
Q3: Buzy Lizzie and Dahlia.
Q4: Strawberry plant.
Q5: House plant that can go outside — Hibiscus 'Alicante'.
Outdoor plants — Strawberry plant and Dahlia.
House plants — Buzy Lizzie and Spider plant.

Page 17 Different Plants Need Different Things
Q1: Water and nutrients.
Q2: Roots.
Q3: The roots anchor it into the ground.
Q4: To support them standing upright.
Q5: Dandelions — "sandy soil" should be ticked.
Marram grass — "sandy soil" should be ticked.
Cattails — "clay soil" should be ticked.

Page 18 Looking at Different Soils
Q1: The two types of soil should look something like this:

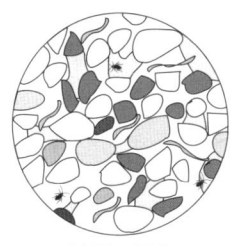 

SANDY SOIL   CLAY SOIL

Q2:

	What colour is the soil?	How dry is the soil?	Any animals?	Any bits of plants?	How much air in the soil?	Any rock particles?
SANDY SOIL	light brown	quite wet	yes	yes	lots	yes
CLAY SOIL	dark brown	very wet	no	no	not much	no

Q3: a) Sandy soil   b) Sandy soil
c) Sandy soil   d) Sandy soil

Page 19 Looking at Different Soils
Q1: The sandy soil was lighter in colour than the clay soil. It was also dryer and had more animals and bits of plants. There were more air gaps in the dry soil and more rock particles too.
Q2: a) Wally's soil.
b) "There are lots of air spaces", "The soil is damp" and "There are dead leaves to feed on" should all be circled.
c) Animals need air spaces in order to breathe. They need water to drink to keep them alive, and they feed on the dead leaves.
Q3: Sandy soil — animals need air spaces in order to breathe, they need water to drink to keep them alive, and they feed on the dead leaves in the soil.

Page 20 Animals and Plants Suit Their Habitats
This page just has information to read for this section.

Page 21 Animals and Plants Suit Their Habitats
Q1: a) It has long, feathery roots to reach as much water as possible.
b) They keep it floating near the surface where there's light.
c) 1. They have hard, waxy shells
2. They hide under rocks to protect themselves.
d) Young blennies are born already able to look after themselves and not in eggs that could be eaten by predators.
e) In the cliff tops there is good protection from predators.

Page 22 Animals and Plants Suit Their Habitats
Q1: Any of the plants and animals can be chosen to write about, as long as there's at least one plant and at least one animal. Here's my choice:

Bladderwrack — Has little sacks of air to keep it floating near to the water surface where there's light.

 Puffin — Eats fish. Can swim using its wings and catch fish with its beak.

 Marram grass — Has long feathery roots to reach water in dry areas.

 Crab — Eats small animals. Is eaten by mackerel. Has a hard shell and hides under rocks to protect itself.

Q2: a) Water plantain grows at the edges of rivers so the flowers are always above the water level.
b) Birds (small birds who shelter under it and pheasants and waterfowl which eat its seeds).

Page 23 More Food Chains
Q1: "Arrows should point from the thing being eaten to the thing doing the eating" should be ticked.

Q2:

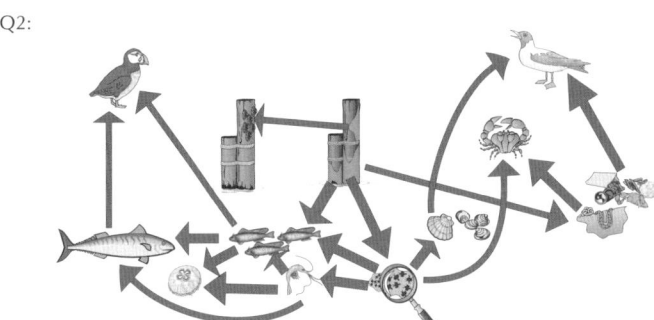

Q3: Algae
Q4: Mackerel
Q5: Shrimp, crab, shellfish, blenny.
Q6: Puffins

Page 24 Big Food Chain Questions
Q1: Here's some examples of correct food chains:

Algae ➡ LUGWORM ➡ CRAB
ALGAE ➡ Zooplankton ➡ SHELLFISH
ZOOPLANKTON ➡ SHRIMP ➡ MACKEREL
ZOOPLANKTON ➡ BLENNY ➡ PUFFIN

Q2: A food chain always starts with a plant which is called the producer. A **PLANT** is an example of a producer. The producer makes food using light, water, air and nutrients. Animals are all **CONSUMERS**, which means that instead of making their own food, they eat plants or other animals. A **SEAGULL** is an example of a consumer. The animals that eat other animals are called **PREDATORS**. An example of this is a **MACKEREL** which eats **BLENNY**. The animal that gets eaten is called the **PREY**. Plants and animals all live in areas that they are suited to, called **HABITATS**.

Page 25 Revision Questions
Q1: 1. Light   2. Air   3. Water   4. Nutrients
Q2: Water and nutrients
Q3: Here's one way to do the key (there are other ways):

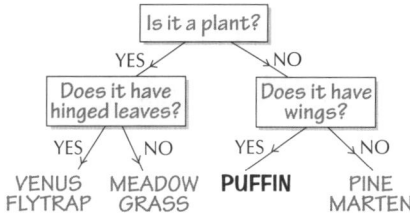

Q4: Giving the plant nutrients.
Q5: Out of a clay and sandy soil the **SANDY** soil is the easiest to dig. The **SANDY** soil has the biggest rock particles and the **CLAY** soil has the least animal and plant bits in it. The **CLAY** soil has smaller air spaces in it and the **SANDY** soil is a good habitat for soil-living animals.
Q6: Anything like this would do: SEEDS ➡ MOUSE ➡ CAT

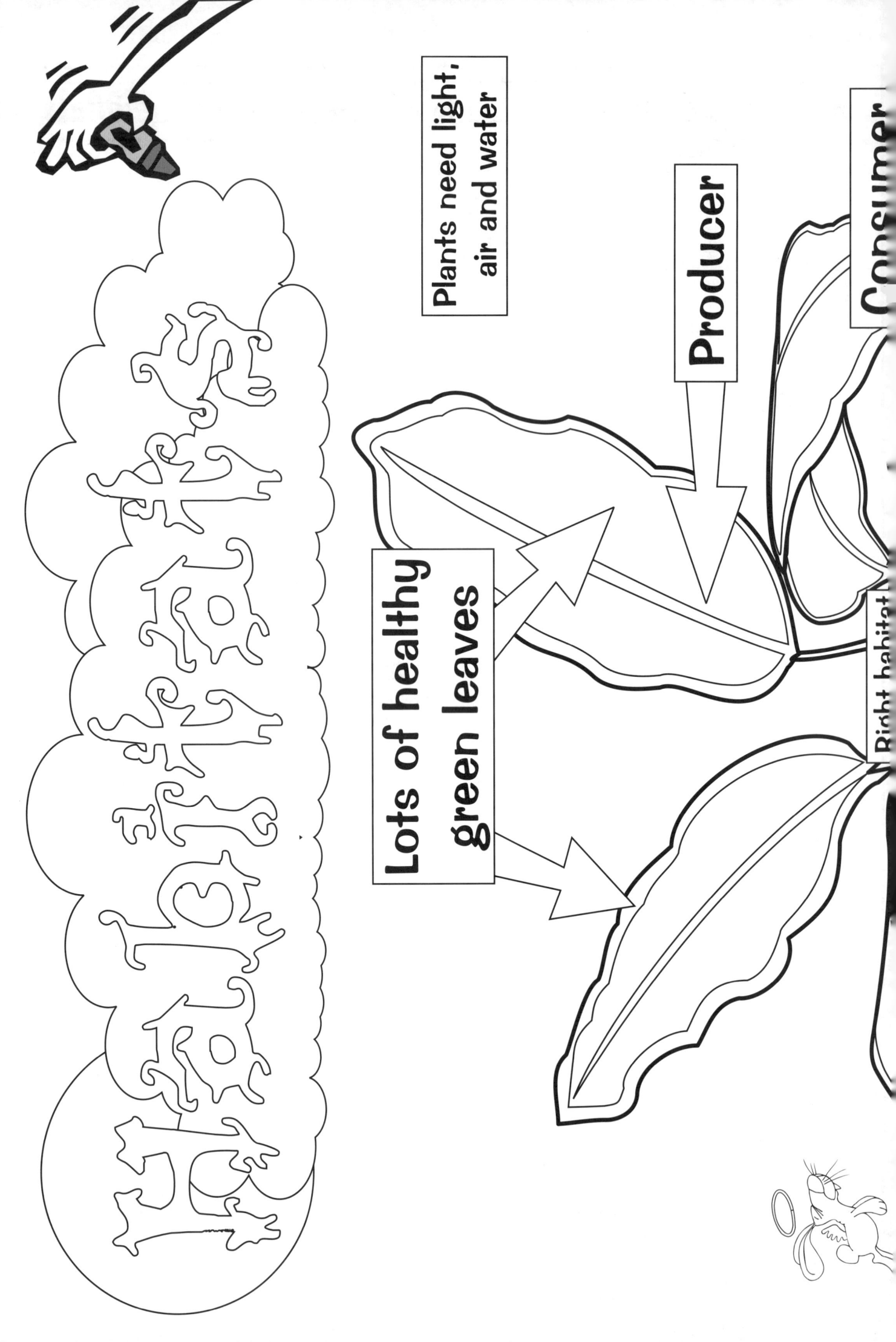

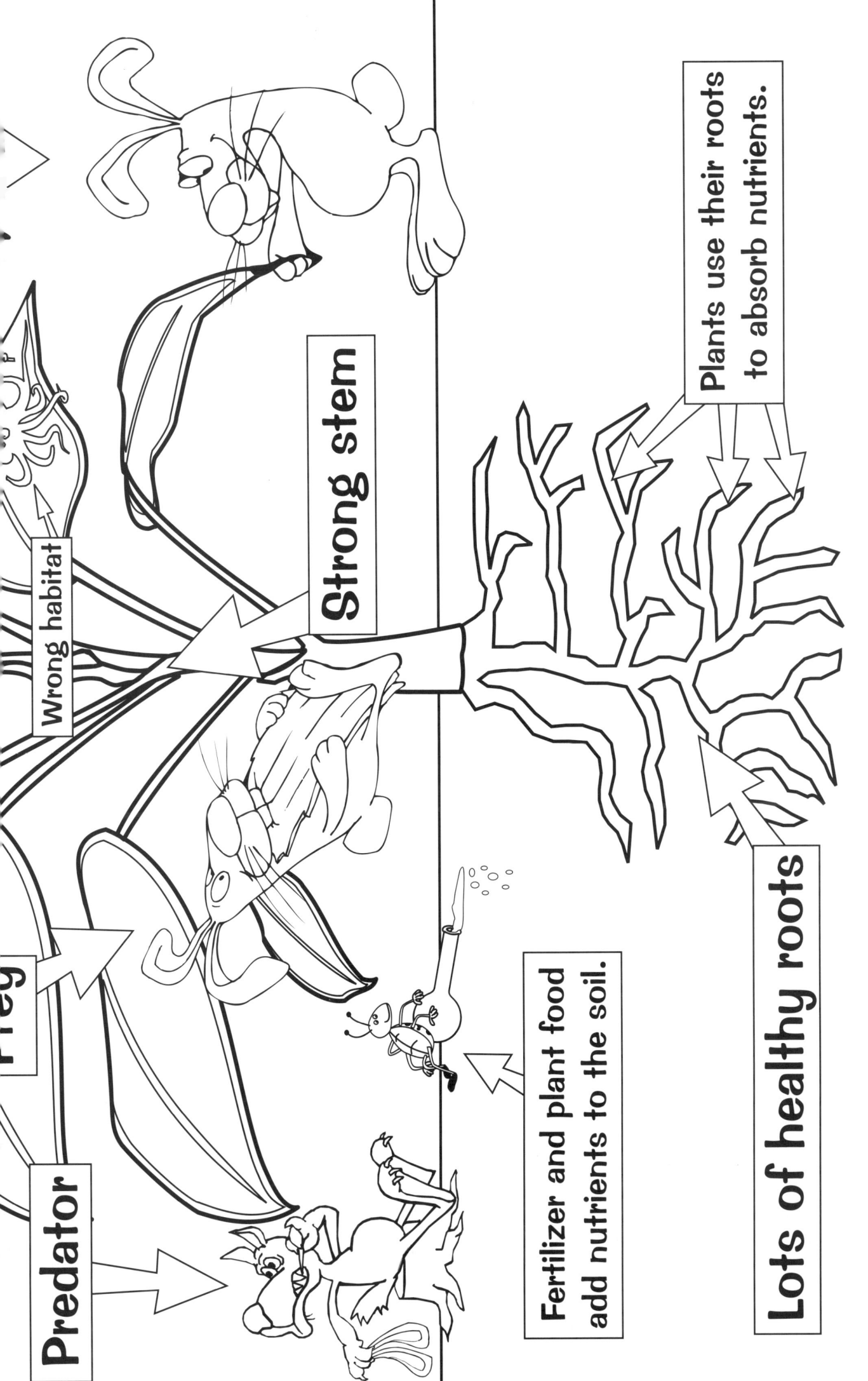

From the CGP KS2 Science Book — Plants and Animals in Their Habitats

PULL OUT ANSWERS AND POSTERPULL OUT ANSWERS AND POSTER***PULL OUT ANSWERS AND POST

KS2 Science Answers — Plants & Animals in Their Habitats

Page 1 Background

Q1:

Q2: The plant that was dying had been in the dark for **TWELVE** weeks. The plant that was in the dark for **THREE** weeks wasn't healthy but should recover. To be healthy, a plant needs **LIGHT**.

Q3: a) Light, air and water.
b) HEALTHY LEAVES   A STRONG STEM   HEALTHY ROOTS

Page 2 What Green Plants Need to Survive

Q1: "Light and warmth", "air" and "water" should be ticked.
Q2: 1. The leaves became healthier.   2. The stem became stronger.
3. The roots became healthier.
Q3: Yes.   Q4: They will all become stronger and healthier again.

Page 3 What Green Plants Need to Survive

Q1: The grass is yellow because it hasn't had any light or air while the plastic sheet was over it.
Q2: The grass would become healthier and turn greener again.
Q3: Plants use **WATER**, **LIGHT** and **AIR** to make new plant material. Plant material is **STEMS**, **ROOTS** and **LEAVES**.

Page 4 What Green Plants Need to Survive

Q1: Leaves.
Q2: Without **LEAVES**, the plant wouldn't be able to make **LIGHT**, **WATER** and **AIR** into products the plant uses to **GROW**.
Q3: a) To grow.   b) From the soil.   c) The roots.
Q4: Nutrients and water.

Page 5 Fertilisers

Q1: Nitrogen, phosphorous pentoxide and potassium oxide.   Q2: Tiny amounts.
Q3: Plants make their own food in their **LEAVES**, using air from all around, water from the **SOIL**, light from the **SUN** and nutrients from the **SOIL**. Animals **CAN'T** make their own food, so they get food by **EATING** plants or other animals.

Page 6 Using Keys

Q1: A — Thistle   B — Perch   C — Flowering Cherry
     D — Puma   E — Pine   F — Woodpecker
     G — Dragonfly   H — Lizard

Page 7 Using Keys

Q1: Print 1 — Dog   Print 2 — Bird   Print 3 — Sheep
     Print 4 — Cat   Print 5 — Horse   Print 6 — Human

Page 8 Using Keys

Q1: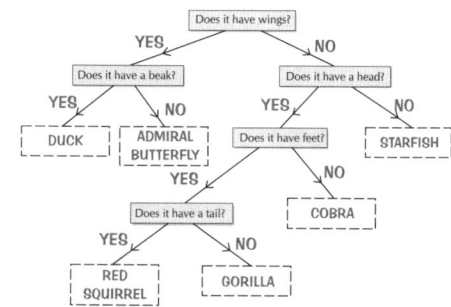

Page 9 Using Keys

Q1: There's lots of possible answers — here's just one of them.

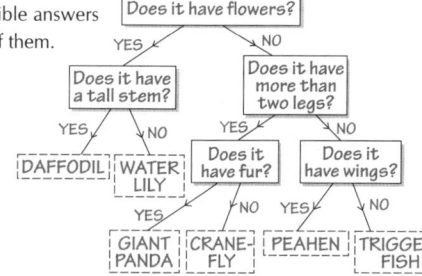

Page 10 Information Overload

All you have to do here is read all the information!

Page 11 Recognising Animals

Q1: Meadow vole   Fox
     Pine marten   Green Woodpecker
     Barn Owl   Meadow Grass
     Squirrel   Oak apple gall wasp
Q2: Galls are strange-looking bumps on trees.
Q3: i) They have a pointed bill and ii) they have a reinforced skull.
Q4: Name of habitat: Oak Tree
    Name of the animals: Green woodpecker & pine marten.
Q5: By passing animals — the seeds stick to their fur and fall off somewhere else.

Page 12 Information Cards — Common Oak

Q1: a) Acorns.
    b) i) Squirrels bury acorns which can grow into new oak trees.
       ii) Animal waste gives nutrients to oak trees.
    c) i) Squirrels eat acorns.
       ii) Squirrels, birds and young gall wasps live in oak trees.
    d) Loses its leaves in Winter.
Q2: Could mention that the galls on oak trees are called 'oak apples', or that pine martens sometimes live in hollows of old oak trees.

Page 13 More Information Cards

Q1: Oak apple gall wasp — Eats galls ('oak apples').
                         — Gets eaten by green woodpeckers.
    Pine marten   — Eats squirrels, rabbits and insects.
                         — Lives in hollows of old trees.
    Squirrel   — Eats acorns.
                         — Gets eaten by pine martens.
                         — Lives in trees.
    Green woodpecker   — Eats insects and larva.
                         — Lives in oak or birch trees.
    Meadow grass   — Pollinated by wind.
                         — Seeds are eaten by meadow voles.
                         — It lives/grows in meadows.
    Meadow vole   — Eats meadow grass and seeds.
                         — Eaten by barn owls and foxes.
                         — Lives in meadows.
    Owl   — Eats meadow voles.
                         — Hunts at night.
                         — Lives in old farm buildings.
    Fox   — Eats rabbits and voles
                         — Lives in dens.

Page 14 Food Chains

Q1: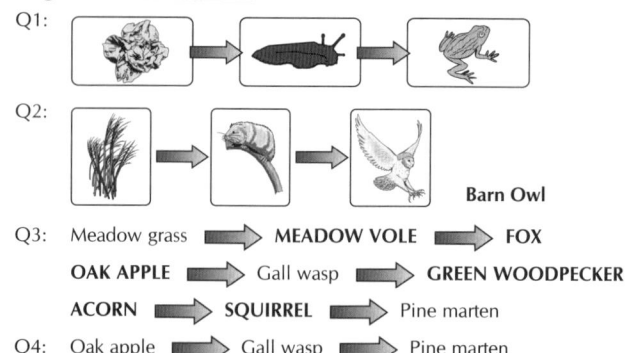

Q2: (Barn Owl)

Q3: Meadow grass ➡ MEADOW VOLE ➡ FOX
    OAK APPLE ➡ Gall wasp ➡ GREEN WOODPECKER
    ACORN ➡ SQUIRREL ➡ Pine marten

Q4: Oak apple ➡ Gall wasp ➡ Pine marten

Page 15 Food Chains

Q1: There are lots of right ways to fill in the table. Here's one way:

Name	Example 1	Example 2
Producer	Meadow Grass	Oak Tree
Consumer	Meadow Vole	Squirrel
Predator	Owl	Fox
Prey	Gall Wasp	Squirrel

PULL OUT ANSWERS AND POSTERPULL OUT ANSWERS AND POSTER***PULL OUT ANSWERS AND POSTE

More Information Cards

Read all the stuff on page 10 before filling in the missing bits on these eight info cards. Make sure you've got it all right — if you don't, you'll fudge up this page and the next.

Q1 Fill all the missing bits (look back to page 10 to find out the facts).

OAK APPLE GALL WASP

When it's young it eats: ....

It gets eaten by: ....

It lives: ....

PINE MARTEN

It eats: ....

....

....

It lives: ....

SQUIRREL

It eats: ....

It gets eaten by: ....

It lives: ....

GREEN WOODPECKER

It eats: ....

....

....

It lives: ....

MEADOW GRASS

It's pollinated by: ....

Its seeds are eaten by: ....

It lives: ....

MEADOW VOLE

It eats: ....

It gets eaten by: .... & ....

It lives: ....

BARN OWL

It eats: ....

Its favourite time for hunting is: ....

It lives: ....

FOX

It eats: ....

....

It lives: ....

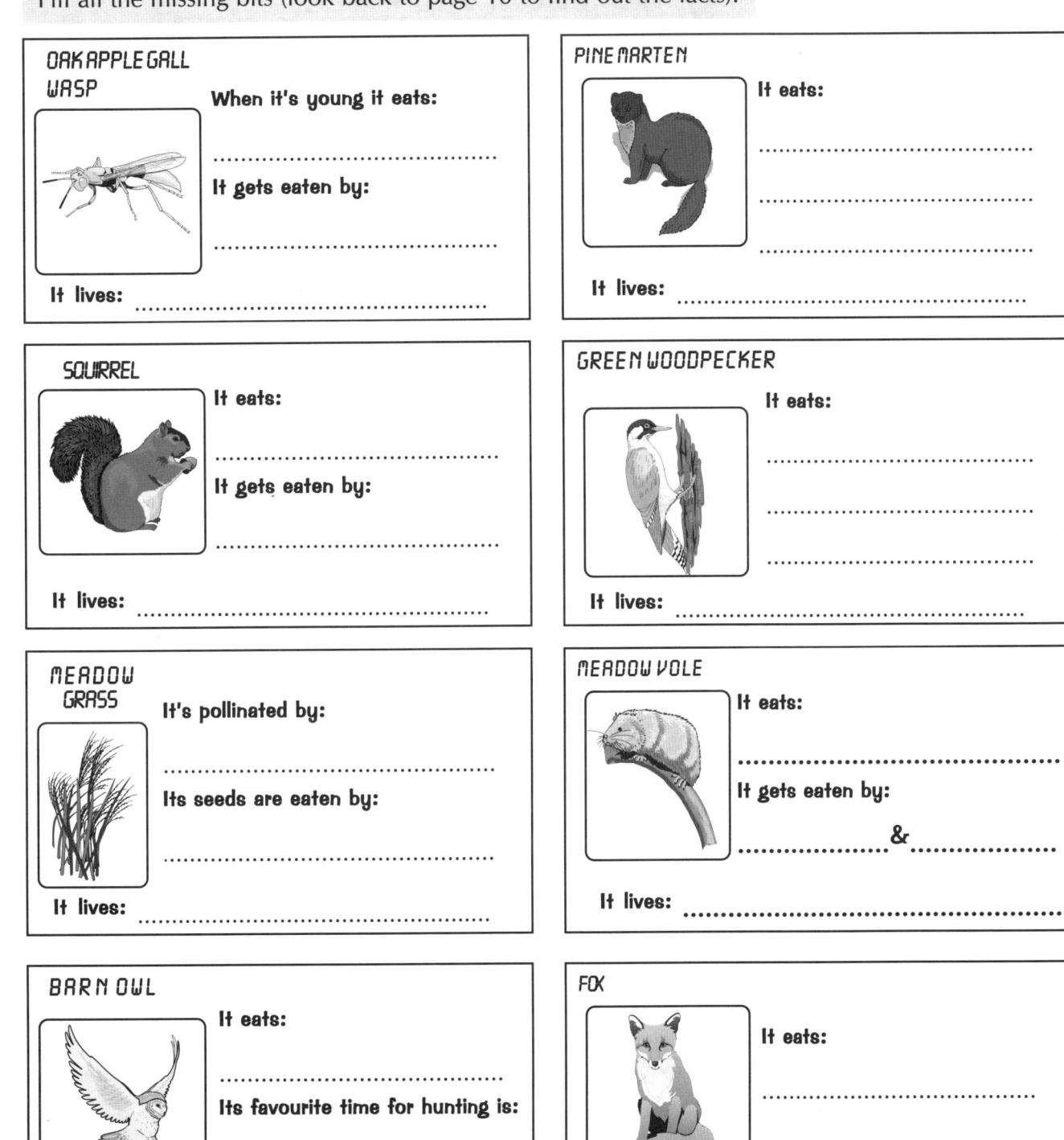

How do you jump a meadow rodent? — vole vault...

"We're close to information overload, Captain — the brain's doing her best, Captain, but if she has to take much more she's gonna blow." "Pull yourself together, set phasers to stun, we're going in."

Food Chains

Here are two 'must-do' rules about drawing food chains: 1) Always start with <u>what's being eaten</u>, 2) Always draw the arrows pointing <u>to</u> the thing doing the eating.

Q1 Put arrows into this food chain to show what is eating what.

Lettuce   Slug   Frog

The food chain was about to change.

Use the information cards on page 13 to help you answer these questions.

Q2 Finish off this food chain with an animal that might eat a vole and draw in the arrows.

Meadow Grass   Meadow Vole   [ ]

Do your best to draw it, but don't spend ages trying to make it perfect.

Q3 Finish the food chains below using organisms from page 13. (Make the 1st different from the one above.)

Meadow Grass → .... → ....

.... → Gall Wasp → ....

.... → .... → Pine Marten

Q4 Use organisms from page 13 to make a food chain that's different from any of the ones above.

.... → .... → ....

<u>Be careful — It's a dog eat dog food world out there...</u>

If you remember those simple rules at the top of the page, food chains are a walk in the park — a park that's eaten by <u>worms</u>, which are eaten by <u>starlings</u>, which are eaten by mad Sam in a big pie...

Food Chains

There are loads of different words people use to talk about what animals do in food chains. You've got to learn four of them — producer, consumer, predator and prey.

Q1 Fill in this table using examples from pages 13 & 10.
(You can have some of the same examples on different rows.)

Name	Description	Example 1	Example 2
Producer	"A producer is any plant at the start of a food chain."	Meadow Grass	....
Consumer	"A consumer is anything that eats something else for food."	....	....
Predator	"A predator is any animal that eats another animal."	....	....
Prey	"Prey is any animal that gets eaten by another animal."	....	....

Q2 Circle the right words from the bracket to complete the paragraph below.

Food chains always (START / END) with a green plant because they

(DO / DON'T) need to eat anything. Green plants make their own

food from (STONES / LIGHT), air, water and (NUTRIENTS / FATS).

Animals need to eat food to survive and don't make their own, so there

is always something (AFTER / BEFORE) them in the food chain.

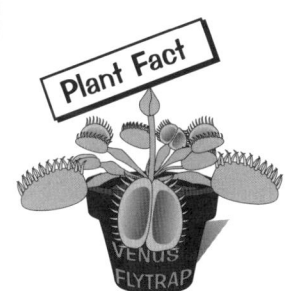

Some plants are a bit different — the Venus Flytrap eats insects.

Q3 Complete the paragraph below using the words prey, predator, producer, consumer.

Food chains always start with a .... Anything in the food chain that

eats something else is a .... An animal that eats another animal is

called a .... An animal that is eaten is called ....

Pie and peas necklace — that's a food chain...

4 fresh new words on this page for you to learn: producer, consumer, predator and prey — you have got to learn what they mean. Otherwise you won't have a clue when you're asked about it.

Different Plants Need Different Things

Plants all need <u>more or less</u> the same kind of things to live — but hey, everyone's a bit different. Some plants prefer the sun, some prefer the shade. Some drink a lot, others don't get so thirsty.

When you buy a plant, you usually get a label stuck in the soil, telling you how to look after it. Have a look at these labels:

Buzy Lizzie (Impatiens schlechteri)
Place out of direct sunlight in a warm place. Water daily to keep soil moist. Feed weekly.

 **STRAWBERRY PLANT**
Place in direct sunlight out of the wind. Ensure soil is kept damp but that water is able to drain away easily. Do not use plant food — this will result in good leaves but not many strawberries.

HIBISCUS 'ALICANTE'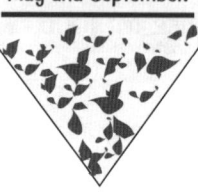
Place in a well-lit place (can be direct sunlight). Water daily and do not allow to dry out. Feed once every 14 days. Can be placed outdoors in a sheltered area between May and September.

SPIDER PLANT
Place in a well-lit room out of direct sunlight. Water daily and do not allow to dry out. Feed once every 4 weeks but do not overfeed.

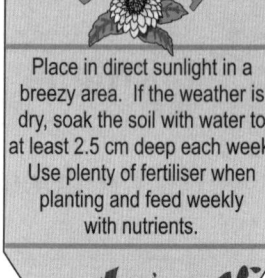 **DAHLIA**
Place in direct sunlight in a breezy area. If the weather is dry, soak the soil with water to at least 2.5 cm deep each week. Use plenty of fertiliser when planting and feed weekly with nutrients.

Q1 Which plants need to be kept out of direct sunlight? ....
and ....

Q2 What does it mean by 'feeding' the plant?

....

Q3 Which two plants need feeding the most often?

.... and ....

Q4 Which plant doesn't need feeding at all?

....

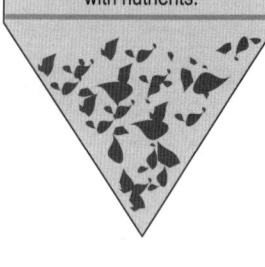

The label said 'Feed plants every day', but Graham got the wrong end of the stick.

Q5 Two of the labels are from outdoor plants, two are from house plants and one is from a house plant that can be put outside for a few months of the year. Which are which?

BY THE WAY: outdoor plants often need plenty of sunlight.

HOUSE PLANT THAT CAN GO OUTSIDE
....

OUTDOOR PLANTS
1) ....
2) ....

HOUSE PLANTS
1) ....
2) ....

House plants? — Is that where houses come from...

It's weird that <u>different plants</u> need such <u>different things</u>. You'd think if you found a good plant fertiliser, it'd be OK for anything, but put it on your strawberry plants and it's <u>bye-bye strawberries</u>.

Different Plants Need Different Things

There's more to <u>plant roots</u> than meets the eye...

Q1 What two things does a plant get from the soil?

.... and ....

Q2 What do they have to pass through to get to the plant?

....

Here's a tree, with its roots showing under the ground.

Q3 How does the tree stay upright?

....

....

Q4 Name one other reason why plants have roots, apart from getting water and nutrients from the soil.

....

Plants that grow in different types of soil have different shaped roots.

In sandy areas there's not much water, so plants there need long roots to reach as much water as possible.

Clay soils hold a lot of water, so plants there only need short roots to get enough water.

Q5 Which soil do you think these plants would grow better in? Tick 'Clay soil' or 'Sandy soil'.

Sandy soil ☐   Clay soil ☐

Dandelions have very long roots.

Marram grass has very long, feathery roots.

Sandy soil ☐   Clay soil ☐

Sandy soil ☐   Clay soil ☐

Cattails have short, thick roots.

The answers are there somewhere — root them out...

There's all this stuff going on underground, but you can't see it. Roots are <u>dead important</u> to plants — that's how they get their <u>nutrients</u>. They're about as important as your mouth is to you.

Looking at Different Soils

MINI-PROJECT

This mini-project is about different types of <u>soil</u> — you're going to try to find out which types are better <u>habitats</u> for animals. You have to look at soils very <u>carefully</u>, using a magnifying glass or microscope, to find out what's in them.

Q1   Find two soil samples — one should be sandy, the other should be clay soil. Look at the soils under a microscope or magnifying glass, and then draw what you see in these two circles.

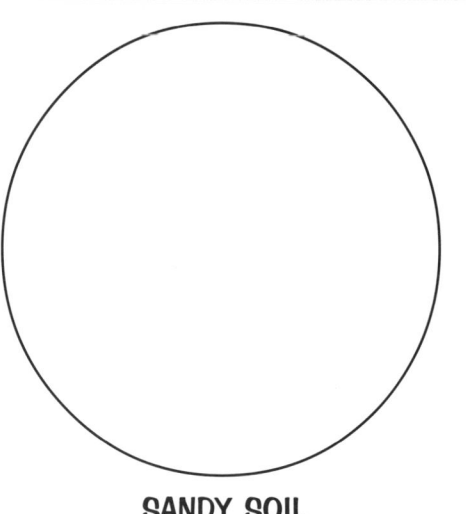

SANDY SOIL   CLAY SOIL

If you can't do the experiment, look at my pictures on page 26.

ALWAYS WASH YOUR HANDS AFTER TOUCHING SOIL.

Ta-da!

Hazel found something better to do with her clay soil.

Q2   Fill in this table with the things that you've seen.

	What colour is the soil?	How dry is the soil?	Any animals?	Any bits of plants?	How much air in the soil?	Any rock particles?
SANDY SOIL						
CLAY SOIL						

Q3 a) Which soil was the easiest to dig up?   ....

   b) Which soil had the largest rock particles?   ....

   c) Which soil had the most animal or plant bits in it?   ....

   d) Which soil had bigger air spaces in it?   ....

Collecting soil samples is cool — <u>ya dig?</u>...

You'd better make sure that your two soils really are <u>different</u>, or your results will be of <u>no use</u> to anyone. And don't forget to wash your hands well afterwards, because soil is pretty dirty.

Looking at Different Soils

Hopefully you've got some stunning soil results — now you can work out what it all means.

Q1 Describe the similarities and differences between the two soils that you tested. Include the things you wrote in the table — how much air they have, how dry they are and so on.

....

....

....

Q2 Wally's garden has damp soil with lots of air spaces and dead leaves in it. The soil in Margaret's garden is very dry, tightly packed and has no leaves and not much air.

a) Whose soil would suit a soil-living animal best? ....

b) Circle three things about that soil that make it suitable for animals to live in.

There are lots of air spaces.   There aren't many air spaces.   There's not much to feed on.   The soil is dry.   The soil is damp.   There are dead leaves to feed on.

c) For each of these things, give a reason why the animal would need it.

....

....

....

Q3 Which of the soil samples you looked at would be a good habitat for soil-living animals? Why?

....

....

...and it comes with a swimming pool...

Ernie's habitat was a cut above the rest.

You can't worm your way out of this one...

Animals and plants manage to live in <u>all sorts</u> of soils — but even so, some soils are <u>better</u> than others for them to live in. Don't hurt any animals (like worms) when you're collecting your soil.

Animals and Plants Suit Their Habitats

Here's an information board about some of the plants and animals that live by the seashore.

HERE AT SILEFARNE BEACH, YOU WILL FIND...

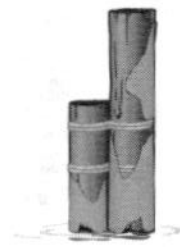

ALGAE (PHYTOPLANKTON**)**

Algae is the common name for microscopic plants. Algae can be found virtually anywhere near the surface of the water — on rocks, bits of wood, in the sand, and floating in the water.

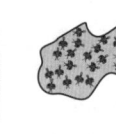

ZOOPLANKTON

Zooplankton is the general name for microscopic animals, such as tiny shrimps, molluscs and larvae of larger animals. They float on or near the surface of the water and feed on algae.

BLADDERWRACK (FUCUS VESICULOSUS**)**

Bladderwrack is a seaweed, which has little sacks of air to keep it floating near the surface where there's light.

MARRAM GRASS (AMMOPHILA ARENARIA**)**

Marram grass belongs to the Graminae family and grows in sandy coastal areas. Marram grass has very long, feathery roots to reach as much water as possible in dry areas.

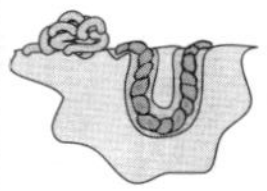

LUGWORM (ARENICOLA MARINA**)**

The lugworm belongs to the Annelid family. Lugworms live in the sand and dig U-shaped burrows. Lugworms feed on microscopic algae in the sand and water. They eat the sand and water, taking what they need out of it and leaving behind a characteristic pile of waste sand which looks like toothpaste that's been squeezed out of a tube.

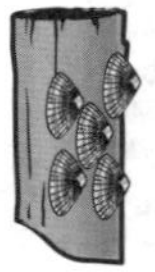

LIMPET (ARCHAEOGASTROPODA**)**

The limpet is an animal with a round, pointed shell, usually found clinging to rocks. Limpets eat vegetation such as algae.

SHELLFISH (PHYLUM MOLLUSCA**)**

Shellfish such as cockles and mussels feed on zooplankton, which they filter out of the water with large gills. They have strong muscles, so they can quickly clamp their shells shut to protect themselves.

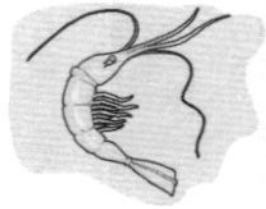

SHRIMP (CRANGON CRANGON**)**

The shrimp can be found in shallow water. Shrimp are hard to see due to their sandy colour, and are often buried up to their eyes in the sand. Shrimp grow to 4-7 cm long, and eat zooplankton.

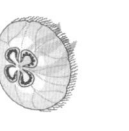  

JELLYFISH (AURELIA AURITA**)**

The jellyfish is a jelly-like invertebrate, usually with stinging tentacles. Jellyfish eat zooplankton, but also catch small creatures such as small fish, shrimp and shellfish, by stinging them with their tentacles.

BLENNY (BLENNIIDAE**)**

The blenny is a small, spiny fish belonging to the Blenniidae family. Blennies eat shrimps, shellfish, zooplankton and algae. Young blennies aren't born in eggs and they're able to look after themselves.

CRAB (CARCINUS MAENAS**)**

Crabs are crustaceans. They have hard, waxy shells and are good at burrowing. They hide under rocks to protect themselves from enemies. Crabs eat small animals, such as lugworms and zooplankton.

MACKEREL (SCOMBER SCOMBRUS**)**

The Atlantic mackerel has a pointed head without scales, and a thick, narrow body covered in tiny scales. It is blue and silver and grows to around 50 cm in length and 1.4 kg in weight. Mackerel swim close to the surface of the sea in large numbers, catching small fish. They also eat shrimp, crabs and shellfish. Mackerel lay their eggs at night, which float on the surface of the water.

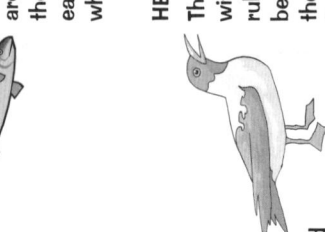

HERRING GULL (LARUS ARGENTATUS**)**

The herring gull is a member of the gull family. It is silver and white, with a yellow bill. Herring gulls will eat almost anything, particularly rubbish and washed up dead sea animals, which they scavenge from beaches. They also eat smaller creatures, such as shellfish, which they carry in their bills and then drop onto rocks to break the shells. Herring gulls nest mainly in the cliff tops, where there is good protection from predators. In winter, they migrate to warmer parts, such as South America and the West Indies.

PUFFIN (FRATERCULA ARCTICA**)**

The puffin is a member of the auk family, and has a big, colourful, triangular bill. The outer layers of the bill are shed after the breeding season. Puffins eat both small and large fish, and catch them by diving below the surface of the water. They snatch fish in their beaks and swim back to the surface, using their wings. The puffin can be found nesting along coastlines in the Northern Hemisphere, although they spend most of their time out at sea and only return to coastlines to breed.

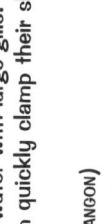 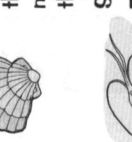

Animals and Plants Suit Their Habitats

There are loads of weird and wonderful animals and plants about — all different shapes and sizes. But one thing they all have in common is that each one needs to be suited to the place it's living.

Q1 This picture shows Silefarne Beach, where you can find all the animals and plants from page 20. Read all about them on the information board, then answer the questions underneath.

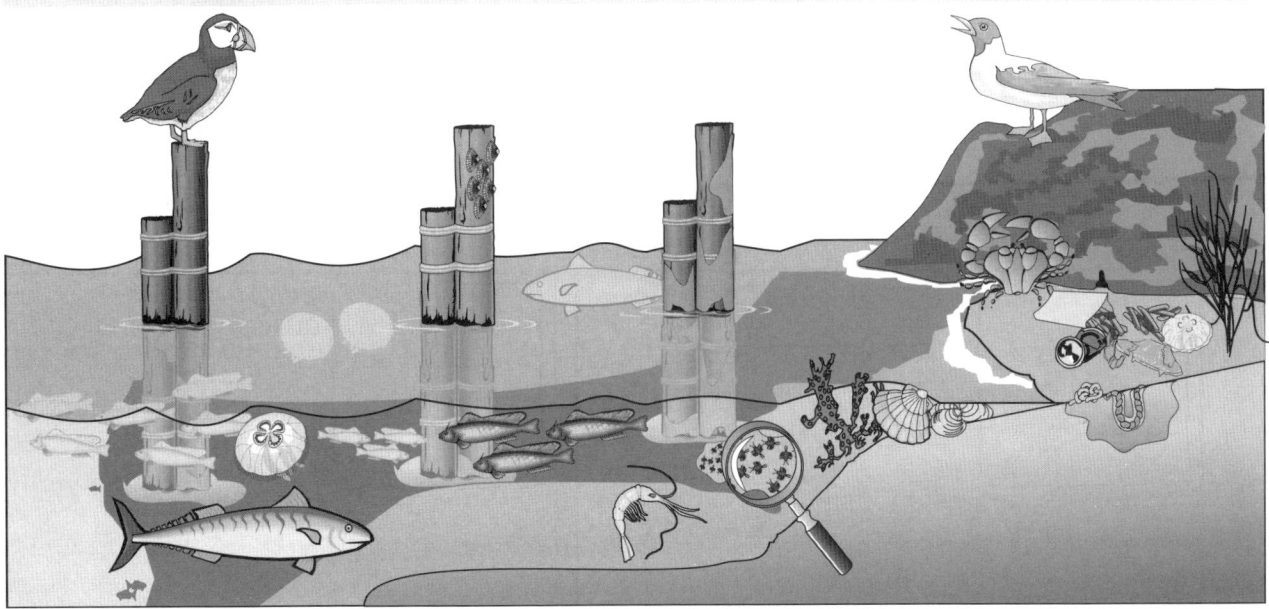

a) How is the marram grass adapted to living in sandy places?

....

b) How do the bladderwrack's sacks of air help it survive?

....

c) Write down two ways the crab is suited to defending itself.

1) ....

2) ....

Jon liked to study underwater life.

d) Most fish lay eggs, which hatch after they are born. How does the way blennies reproduce mean that their young are better protected from predators from the moment they're born?

....

....

e) The herring gull is suited to living by the sea, because it can eat sea animals that get washed up on the beach. Find another reason the gull is suited to living by the shore.

....

A Blenny for your thoughts...

Plants and animals live in particular places for good reasons — they'd find it hard to survive anywhere else. Puffins wouldn't live inland, because there wouldn't be many fish for them to eat.

Animals and Plants Suit Their Habitats

All the plants and animals on page 20 are <u>adapted</u> to their seashore habitat in some way. You'll need to pick out the four most interesting ones for this page.

Q1 Make information cards for four of the plants and animals from page 20. (Use at least one plant and at least one animal.) For each one you need to include these things:

Animal:
1. What the animal eats.
2. What animals eat it (if any).
3. One way it's adapted to its habitat.
4. Draw a picture of the animal.

Plant:
1. What animals eat it (if any).
2. One way it's adapted to its habitat.
3. Draw a picture of the plant.

Got that? OK, now you can get started...

There are some information cards on pages 14 and 15, to show you how they should look.

Q2 Look at this article I found in "Freshwater Weekly", then answer the questions next to it.

Britain's Riverside Beauty

Britain's rivers are home to a wide range of plants — but none more delicate and beautiful than the water plantain. The water plantain's tiny flowers have just 3 white and purple petals, which rarely last for more than a day — and you will only see them open during afternoons and early evenings. Once the flowers disappear, they are replaced by flat nutlets of seeds, which are eaten by pheasants and waterfowl. The plant itself grows in shallow water at the edges of rivers and provides good shelter for many smaller birds. Water plantain can grow up to 1 m high, which means that it can still reproduce even if the water level rises, because its seeds are still above the water level for birds to eat.

a) How does the water plantain make sure it reproduces, even if the water level rises?

....

....

b) If water plantain ever died out, which creatures would suffer?

....

I'm not suited to this habitat — a beach in Greece would suit me...

Habitats, habitats... there are loads of the things. Just when you thought you'd got the sea shore mastered, I go and throw in a river. Oh well — that's just the way it goes. You love it really.

More Food Chains

More food chain stuff, but this time it's a tad harder. Use the information on page 20 to help you.

Q1 Which way should the arrows point in a food chain? Tick the right answer below.

Arrows should point from the thing being eaten to the thing doing the eating. ☐

Arrows should point from the thing doing the eating to the thing being eaten. ☐

Q2 Draw arrows on the picture below to show what eats what. *(Tip: There are more than 15 arrows to draw.)*

The picture will end up showing lots of food chains all over the place. Don't panic — this is called a "food web", which you're not meant to learn until next year, but I reckon you can handle it.

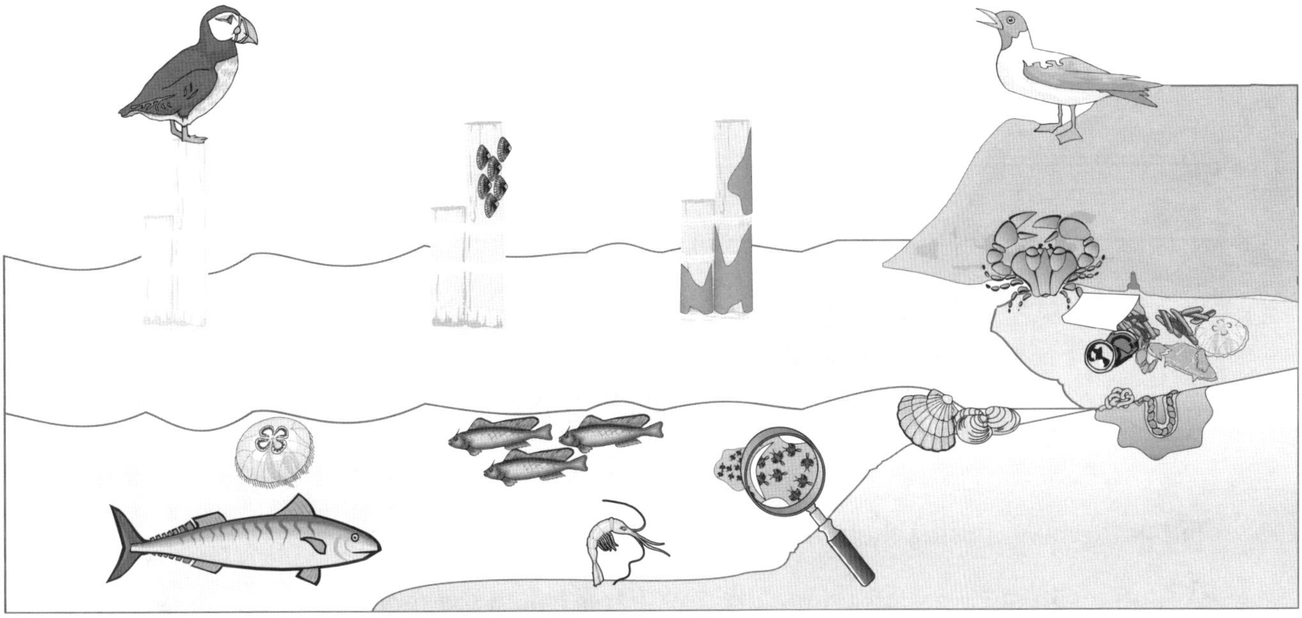

Q3 Name the producer from the picture above. ....

Q4 Name one predator from the picture above. ....

Q5 Name four organisms that eat zooplankton.

....

....

Q6 What might starve if all the fish in the sea disappeared?

....

I'M THE ONLY PRODUCER ROUND HERE BUSTER!

Producer

Everyone was about to see Daisy's nasty side.

Why is the beach wet? — Because the sea weed...

You've done food chains once already in this book so these pages should be as simple as falling... and hopefully involve a lot less pain. Remember: <u>food web</u> = a load of <u>food chains</u> stuck together.

Big Food Chain Questions

Two big questions for you to do here — take your time and use pages 20 and 24 to help you.
There's blenny to do so I'll clam up and stop huffing and puffin at you.

Q1 Use the boxes below to write out some of the different food chains from the picture on page 23. Put all the arrows in as well and make sure they are pointing the right way.

| Algae | → | .... | → | .... |

| .... | Zooplankton | .... |

| .... | .... | .... |

| .... | .... | .... | .... |

Q2 Fill in the blanks using the power of your mind alone (oh... and a pen).

A food chain always starts with a plant which is called the producer.

A .... is an example of a producer. The producer makes food using light, water, air and nutrients. Animals are all .... , which means that instead of making food, they eat plants or other animals. A .... is an example of a consumer. The animals that eat other animals are called ....

An example of this is a .... which eats ....

The animal that gets eaten is called the ....

Plants and animals all live in areas that they are suited to, called ....

Voles hate bionic owls.

C = "Big blue wobbly thing that mermaids live in"...

To get food chains right, always start with what's <u>being</u> eaten and draw the arrow pointing to what's <u>eating</u> it. And remember that the predator <u>ISN'T</u> always bigger than the prey. (E.g. buffalo → tiger.)

Revision Questions

It's page 25 and you still want more — well, this truckload of questions should sort you out.

Q1   Name the four things a plant needs to survive.   1) ....

2) ....   3) ....   4) ....

Q2   Name the two things a plant sucks up through its roots.   .... & ....

Q3   Finish the questions in this key so it can be used to find the names of these four organisms. Then fill in the names — if you can't remember them, look back through the book to help you.

Is it a plant?
YES ↙   ↘ NO

YES ↙   ↘ NO   YES ↙   ↘ NO
                                      PUFFIN

....

....

Q4   What do plant labels mean by 'feeding' the plant?   ....

....

Q5   Use the words 'clay' and 'sandy' to finish this paragraph about clay and sandy soils.

Out of a clay and sandy soil the .... soil is the easiest to dig.

The .... soil has the largest rock particles and the .... soil

has the least plant and animal bits in it. The .... soil has smaller air spaces in

it and the .... soil is a good habitat for soil-living animals.

Q6   Fill in the boxes below to make a food chain that doesn't appear anywhere in this book.

[..................] ➡ [..................] ➡ [..................]

On a Nun's back — a habit's habitat...
Animals and plants all live, eat, drink and die in places they're suited to, called habitats — that's that.

Index

A
acorns 12
admiral butterfly 8
algae 20, 24
animal footprints 7
arrows - food chains 14, 23

B
barn owl 10, 11, 13
bionic owls 24
bladderwrack 20, 21
blenny 20, 21, 23
bumble bees 10

C
cattails 17
clay soils 17, 18
cobra 8
common oak 12
consumer 15, 24
crab 20, 21, 23

D
daffodil 9
dandelions 17
deciduous trees 12
distribution of meadow grass seeds 11
dragonfly 6
duck 8

E
experiment
   experiment on school lawn 3
   experiment to see if plants need light 1
   experiment with my sister's plant 2
   mini-project - looking at different soils 18-19

F
feeding plants 16
fertiliser (or fertilizer) 4-5
fish 20, 21, 23
flowering cherry 6
food - plant food 5
food chains 14, 15, 23, 24
food web 23
footprints - animal 7
foxes 10, 11, 13
frog 14

G
gall wasp 10, 11, 13, 14
galls 10, 11
giant panda 9

gorilla 8
green plants 1-5, 15-17
green woodpecker 10, 11, 13, 14

H
habitats 10-11, 18-23, 25
herring gull 20

I
information cards 12, 13 22

J
jellyfish 20, 23

K
keys 6-9

L
labels on plants 1, 16
leaves 1-5, 19
lettuce 14
limpet 20
lizard 6
lugworm 20, 23

M
mackerel 20, 23
marram grass 17, 20
material - plant material 4
meadow grass 10-11, 13-15
meadow vole 10-11, 13-15
mini-project - looking at different soils 18-19

N
nasty chemicals in fertiliser 5
nutrients 4-5, 15, 17, 24

O
oak apple gall wasps 10, 11, 13, 14
oak 10, 12

P
peahen 9
perch 6
pine 6
pine marten 10-11, 13-14
plants 1-5, 15-17
   plants kept in the dark and light 1
   what plants need to be healthy 1-4, 16-17
   plant food and fertiliser 5
   plant labels 1, 16
   plant material 4
plastic sheets 3

predator 15, 23
prey 15
producer 15, 23, 24
puffin 20, 23
puma 6

R
rabbits 10, 12
red squirrel 8
roots - plant roots suck nutrients 4, 17
   plants need healthy roots 1
   tree roots 17

S
sheets of plastic 3
shellfish 20, 23
shrimp 20, 23
slug 14
soil 4-5, 16-19
   clay soils 17, 18
   sandy soils 17, 18
squirrels 10-13
   red squirrel 8
starfish 8
starlings 14

T
testing
   mini-project - looking at different soils 18-19
thistle 6
tree roots 17
triggerfish 9

V
voles - meadow voles 10-14

W
wasps - oak apple gall 10, 11
water 1-4, 16-17, 25
water lily 9
water plantain 22
woodpecker 6
   green woodpecker 10-14

Z
zooplankton 20, 23, 24

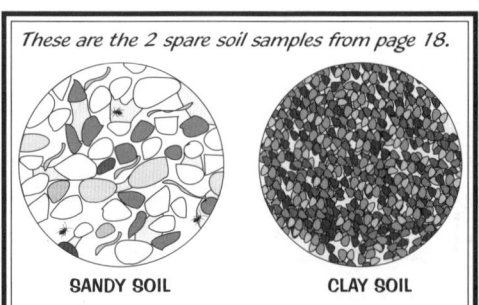
These are the 2 spare soil samples from page 18.
SANDY SOIL   CLAY SOIL